HERON DANCE

Address Book

A friendship can weather most things and thrive in thin soil; but it needs a little mulch of letters and phone calls and small, silly presents every so often.

Pam Brown

This book belongs to:

Let the beauty we love be what we do.
Rumi

Heron Dance Press and Art Studio
179 Rotax Road
N. Ferrisburg, VT 05473
www.herondance.org
888-304-3766

Printed in China

Heron Dance donates art to dozens of grassroots wilderness protection groups each year. In addition, Heron Dance supports the Northeast Wilderness Trust with financial donations

ISBN: 1-933937-10-6

Edited by Ann O'Shaughnessy
Cover art and illustrations by Roderick MacIver of Heron Dance

For information about special discounts for bulk purchases, please contact Ingram Publisher Services at 800-961-7698

Emergency information

Police

Fire

Ambulance

Hospital

Poison control

Work

Doctors

Neighbors

Relatives

Other

Frequently Called Numbers

Name	Number

Name & Address | Numbers

A

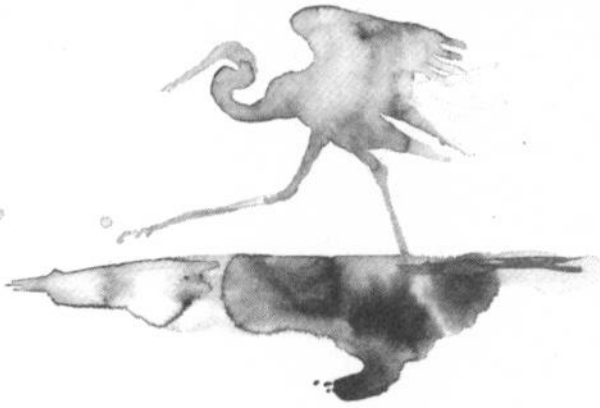

Name & Address	Numbers

Name & Address	Numbers

Name & Address	Numbers

Name & Address	Numbers

Name & Address	Numbers

B

Name & Address	Numbers

B,

Marcelo & Tita Buenviaje
Blk 1 Lot 10 Sandigan Homeowners Assn
M. Santos Ext Antipolo City
Philippines 1870

Name & Address	Numbers

B

Name & Address	Numbers

Name & Address	Numbers

Name & Address	Numbers

B

Name & Address	Numbers

Name & Address | Numbers

C

C

Name & Address	Numbers

Name & Address	Numbers

Name & Address	Numbers

Name & Address	Numbers

C

Name & Address	Numbers

Name & Address | Numbers

D

D

Name & Address	Numbers

Name & Address	Numbers

Name & Address | Numbers

Name & Address	Numbers

Name & Address	Numbers

Name & Address | Numbers

E

E

Name & Address	Numbers

Name & Address	Numbers

Name & Address	Numbers

Name & Address	Numbers

F

Name & Address	Numbers

Name & Address	Numbers

Name & Address	Numbers

Name & Address	Numbers

Name & Address	Numbers

Name & Address | Numbers

G

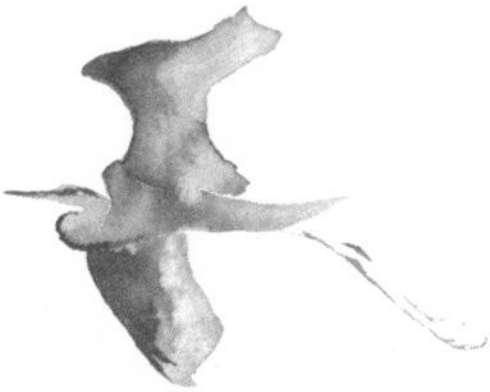

Name & Address	Numbers

Name & Address	Numbers

Name & Address	Numbers

Name & Address	Numbers

Name & Address	Numbers

Name & Address	Numbers

H

Name & Address	Numbers

Name & Address	Numbers

Name & Address	Numbers

Name & Address	Numbers

Name & Address	Numbers

Name & Address	Numbers

I

Name & Address	Numbers

Name & Address	Numbers

Name & Address	Numbers

Name & Address	Numbers

J

Name & Address	Numbers

Name & Address	Numbers

Name & Address	Numbers

Name & Address	Numbers

K

Name & Address	Numbers

Name & Address	Numbers

Name & Address	Numbers

Name & Address	Numbers

Name & Address	Numbers

Name & Address	Numbers

L

Name & Address	Numbers

Name & Address	Numbers

Name & Address	Numbers

Name & Address	Numbers

Name & Address	Numbers

Name & Address	Numbers

M

Name & Address	Numbers

Name & Address	Numbers

Name & Address	Numbers

Name & Address	Numbers

Name & Address	Numbers

Name & Address	Numbers

N

Name & Address	Numbers

Name & Address	Numbers

Name & Address	Numbers

Name & Address | Numbers

O

Name & Address	Numbers

Name & Address	Numbers

Name & Address	Numbers

Name & Address | Numbers

P

P

Name & Address	Numbers

Name & Address	Numbers

P

Name & Address	Numbers

Name & Address	Numbers

Name & Address	Numbers

Name & Address	Numbers

Q

Q

Name & Address	Numbers

Name & Address	Numbers

R

Name & Address	Numbers

Name & Address	Numbers

R

Name & Address

Numbers

Name & Address	Numbers

R

Name & Address	Numbers

Name & Address | Numbers

S

Name & Address	Numbers

Name & Address	Numbers

S

Name & Address	Numbers

Name & Address	Numbers

Name & Address	Numbers

Name & Address	Numbers

T

Name & Address	Numbers

Name & Address	Numbers

T

Name & Address	Numbers

Name & Address	Numbers

T

Name & Address	Numbers

Name & Address	Numbers

U

Name & Address	Numbers

Name & Address	Numbers

V

V

Name & Address	Numbers

Name & Address	Numbers

V

Name & Address	Numbers

Name & Address	Numbers

W

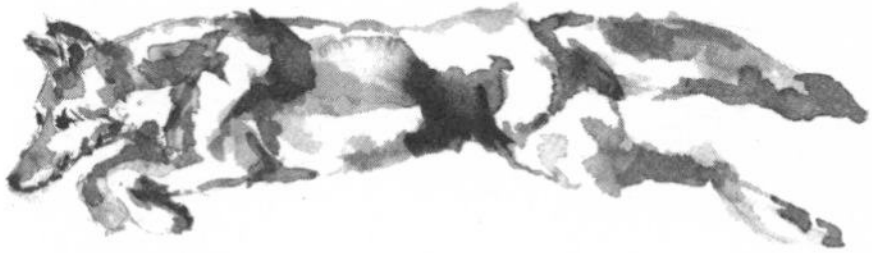

W

Name & Address	Numbers

Name & Address	Numbers

W

Name & Address	Numbers

Name & Address	Numbers

X

Name & Address	Numbers

Name & Address | Numbers

Y

Name & Address	Numbers

Name & Address	Numbers

Z

Name & Address	Numbers

Name & Address	Numbers

HERON DANCE
Press & Art Studio

A big thank you to all who have supported our efforts to publish work that celebrates the gift of life, the beauty of the natural world, and the goodness of which humans are capable.

Heron Dance Press & Art Studio explores diverse perspectives on the human search for meaning, creativity, and the human connection to the natural world. In addition to wilderness classics, books of inspiration, daybooks, phone & address books, and blank journals, we also sell original artwork, limited-edition prints, and notecards. We publish a quarterly journal and offer a free weekly email, *A Pause for Beauty*.

Ann O'Shaughnessy, Editor

Ann O'Shaughnessy joined Heron Dance Press in 2000, bringing with her a love of words and wild nature and a passion for the Heron Dance mission: to provide "art, words, and good company for the seeker's journey." She leads Wild Soul workshops—an exploration of efforts to live our truth.

Roderick MacIver, Artist

Born in Canada, Roderick MacIver currently splits his time between Vermont and his studio in New York's Adirondacks. His work is inspired by a love of wild nature. Readers and art patrons write hundreds of letters a year to Heron Dance responding to the sense of peace and serenity embodied in his watercolors. Roderick MacIver founded Heron Dance Press & Art Studio in 1995 to celebrate the seeker's journey and the spirit and beauty of all that is wild.